# Opposites
# Color, Trace, and Learn

above

below

This book belongs to

Eric — 5

Frank Schaffer Publications, Inc.

# Short

short

# Long

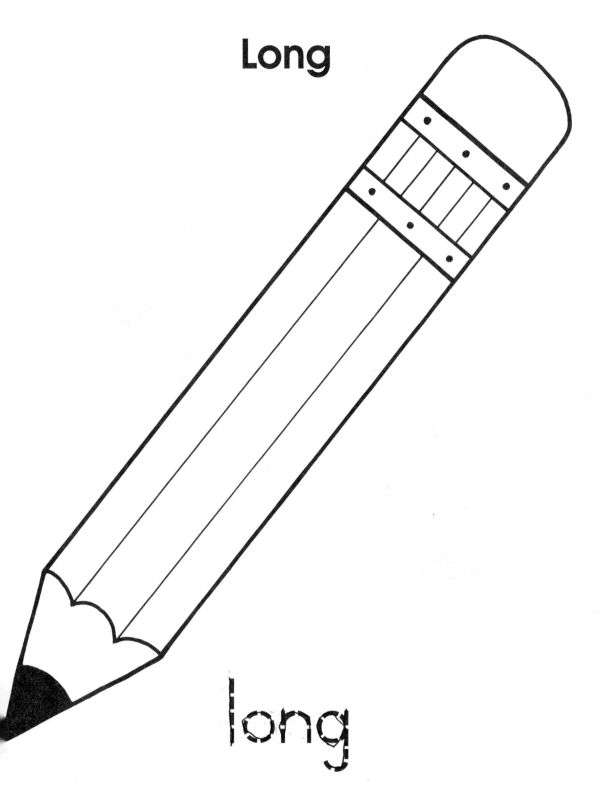

long

# Up

up

4

# Down

down

# Over

over

# Under

## under

# Above

above

# Below

below

FS-8187 HH—Opposites: Color, Trace, and Learn

# Full

full

FS-8187 HH—Opposites: Color, Trace, and Lea

# Empty

empty

FS-8187 HH—Opposites: Color, Trace, and Learn

# Open

open

# Closed

closed

# Hot

hot

    14    

# Cold

cold

# New

new

16

FS-8187 HH—Opposites: Color, Trace, and Lea

# Old

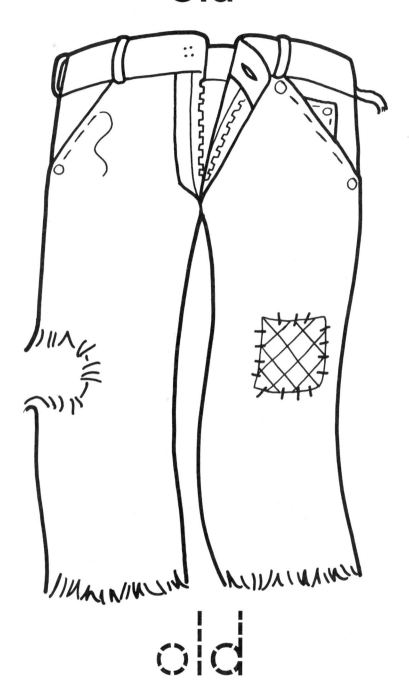

old

# Clean

clean

# Dirty

dirty

# Dry

dry

20

# Wet

wet

# Big

big

FS-8187 HH—Opposites: Color, Trace, and Lea

# Little

In

in

FS-8187 HH—Opposites: Color, Trace, and Lea

# Out

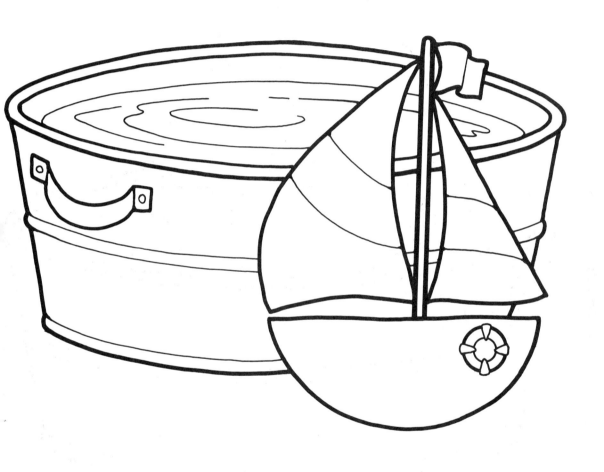

out

FS-8187 HH—Opposites: Color, Trace, and Learn

# Front

front

FS-8187 HH—Opposites: Color, Trace, and Lear

Remove the puppet pages from the book. Help your child color, cut out, and assemble the finger puppets. Have your child match the opposite puppets.

B

FS-8187 HH— Opposites: Color, Trace, and Lea

C

FS-8187 HH— Opposites: Color, Trace, and Learn

D

# Back

back

# Push

push

# Pull

pull

# Slow

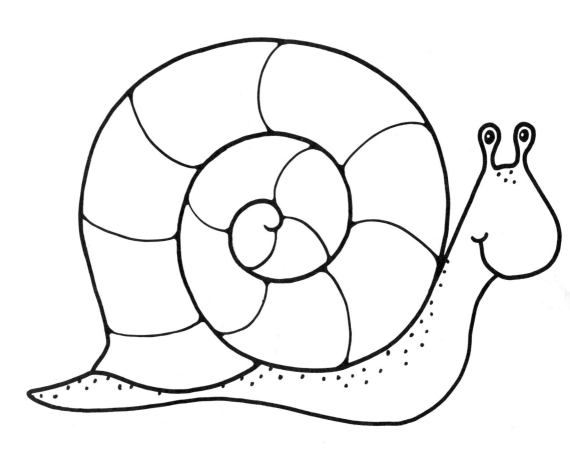

slow

# Fast

fast

# On

## on

# Off

# Happy

happy

# Sad

sad

# Sit

## sit

# Stand

stand

# Night

night

38 FS-8187 HH—Opposites: Color, Trace, and Lea

# Day

day

# Near

near

# Far

far

# Stop

stop

 FS-8187 HH—Opposites: Color, Trace, and Lea

# Go

go

43

FS-8187 HH—Opposites: Color, Trace, and Learn

# Right

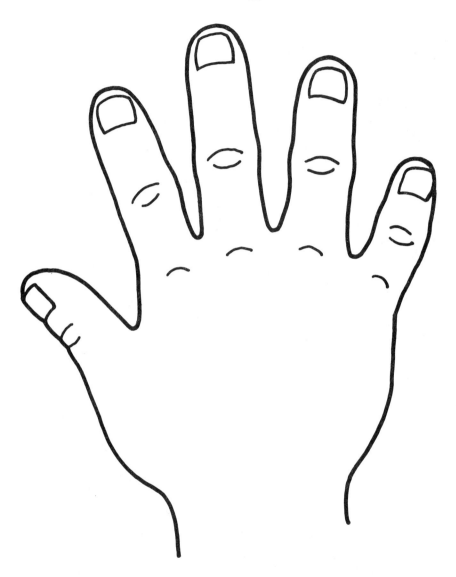

right

# Left

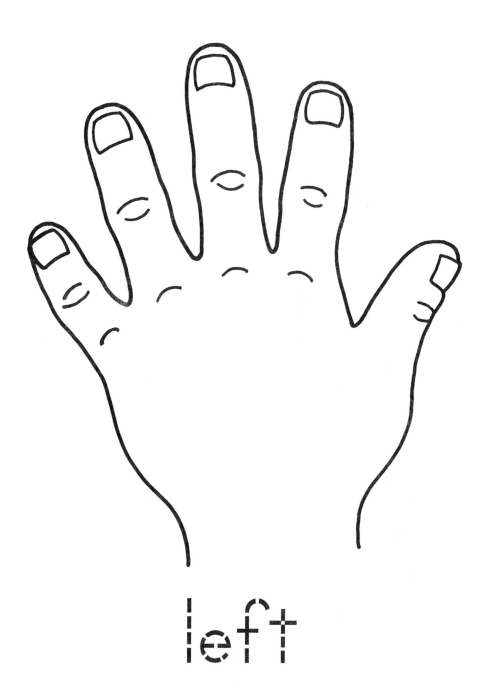

left

# Top

top

46

# Bottom

bottom

# Inside

inside

# Outside

outside

# Summer

summer

50

FS-8187 HH—Opposites: Color, Trace, and Le

# Winter

winter

# Match the pictures that are opposites